# 2012 GREATEST Pop & MOVIE Hits

W9-AUF-649

## Arranged by Dan Coates

THE BIGGEST HITS ★ THE GREATEST ARTISTS

## CONTENTS

2012

**ALFRED**

Produced by
Alfred Music Publishing Co., Inc.
P.O. Box 10003
Van Nuys, CA 91410-0003
alfred.com

Printed in USA.

ISBN-10: 0-7390-9050-X
ISBN-13: 978-0-7390-9050-3

 **Alfred Cares.** Contents printed on 100% recycled paper.

# THE BIG BANG THEORY

## (Main Title Theme)

Words and Music by Ed Robertson
Arranged by Dan Coates

# COUGH SYRUP

Words and Music by
Sameer Gadhia, Eric Cannata, Jacob Tilley,
Francois Comtois and Ehson Hashemian
Arranged by Dan Coates

*Chorus:*

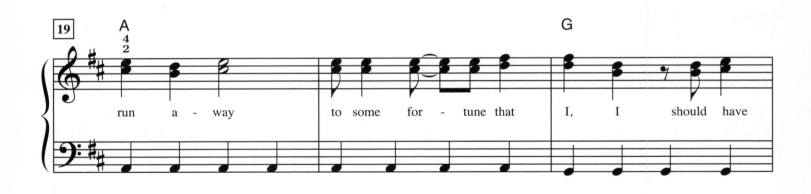

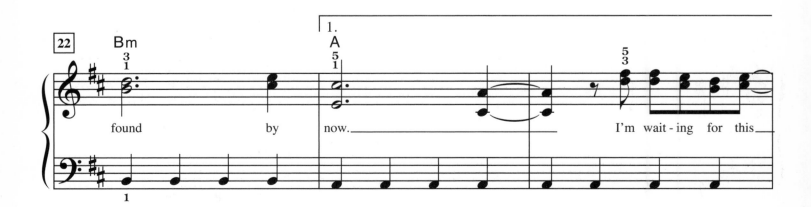

# EXTREMELY LOUD & INCREDIBLY CLOSE

## (Main Theme)

By Alexandre Desplat
Arranged by Dan Coates

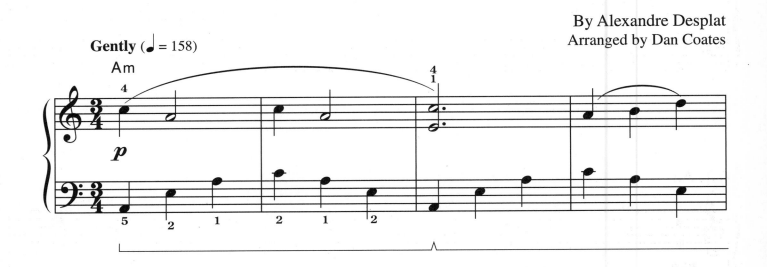

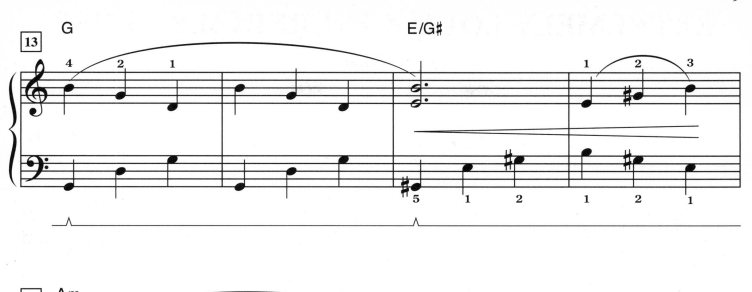

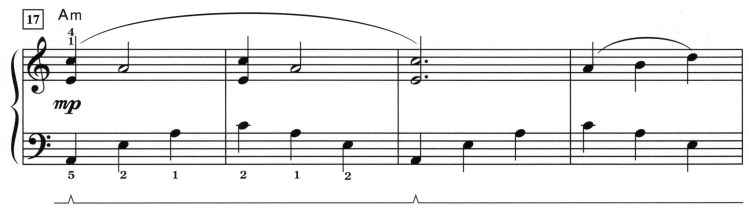

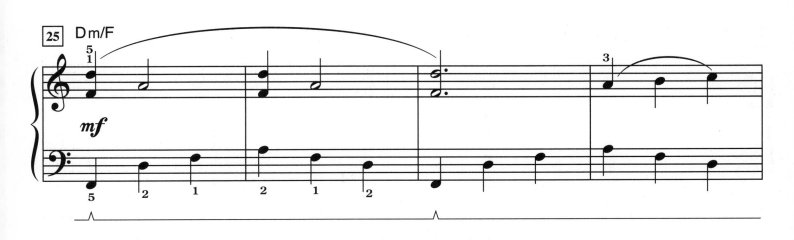

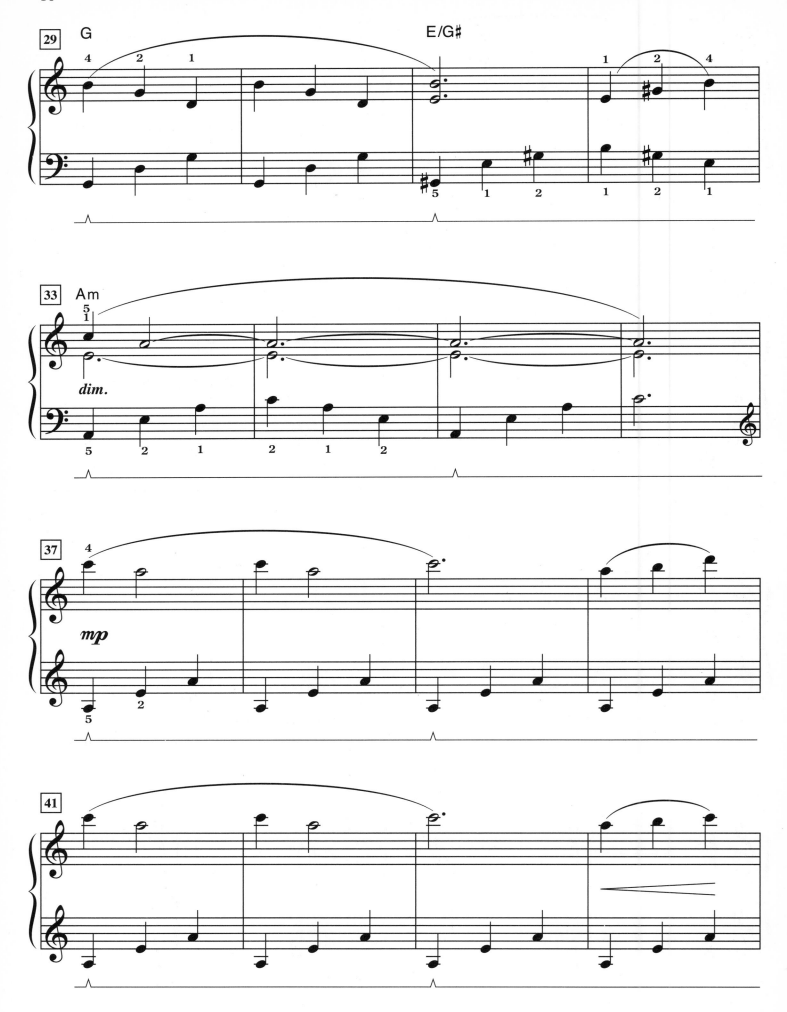

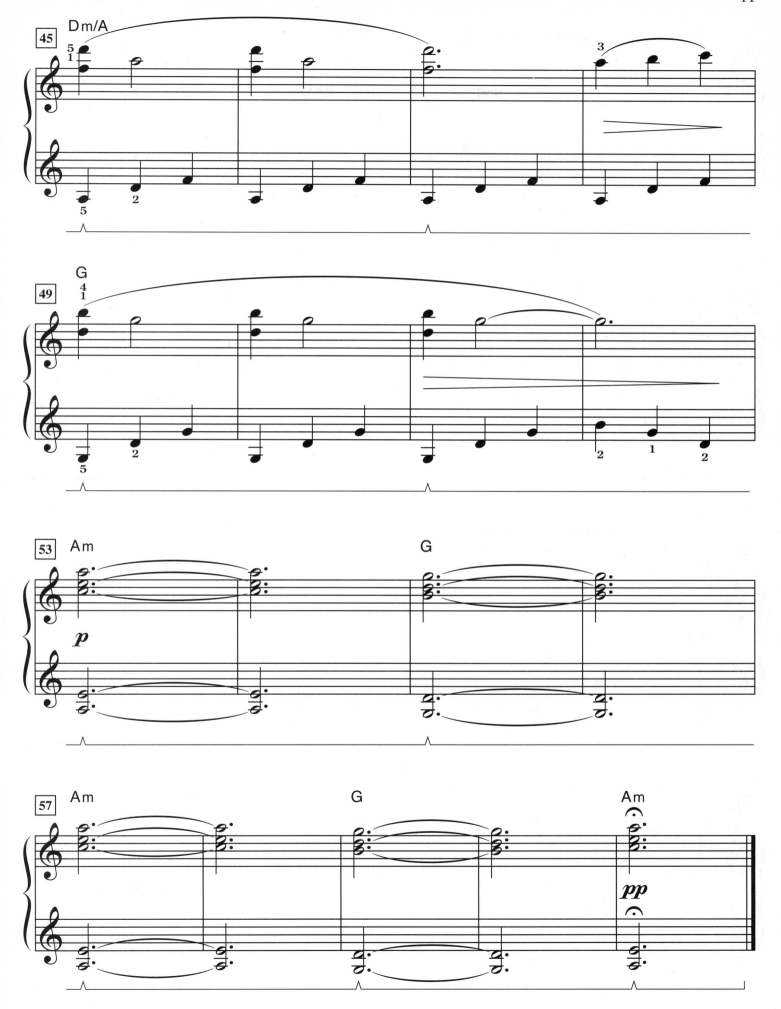

# GOOD GIRL

Words and Music by
Carrie Underwood, Ashley Gorley and Chris DeStefano
Arranged by Dan Coates

**Moderately, with a country rock beat** ( ♩ = 132 )

*Verse:*

1. Hey, good girl, with your head in the clouds, I
2. *See additional lyrics*

bet you I can tell you what you're think-in' a-bout.__ You'll see a good boy, gon-na

give you the world.__ But he's gon-na leave you cry-in' with your heart in the dirt.__ His

lips are drip-pin' hon-ey, but he'll sting you like a bee.__ So, lock up all your love and go and

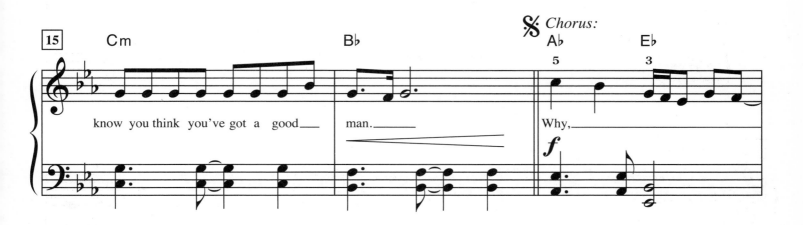

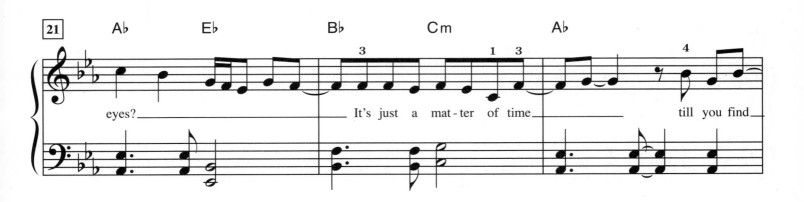

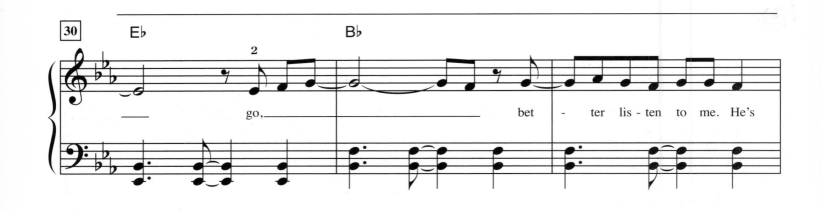

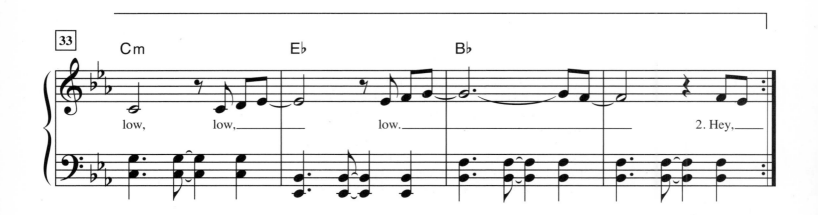

*Verse 2:*
Hey, good girl, you got a heart of gold,
You want a white wedding and a hand you can hold.
Just like you should, girl, like every good girl does,
Want a fairy tale ending, somebody to love.
But he's really good at lyin', yeah, he'll leave you in the dust,
Cuz' when he says forever, well it don't mean much.
Hey, good girl, so good for him.
Better back away honey, you don't know where he's been.
*(To Chorus:)*

# HERE'S TO US

Words and Music by
Lizzy Hale, Toby Gad and Danielle Brisebois
Arranged by Dan Coates

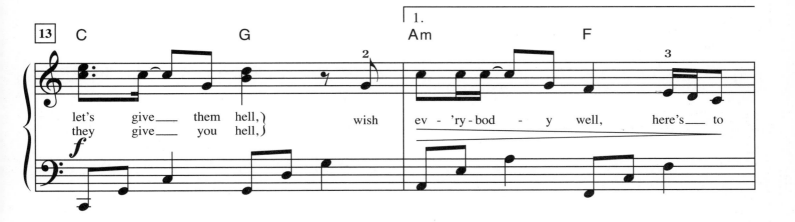

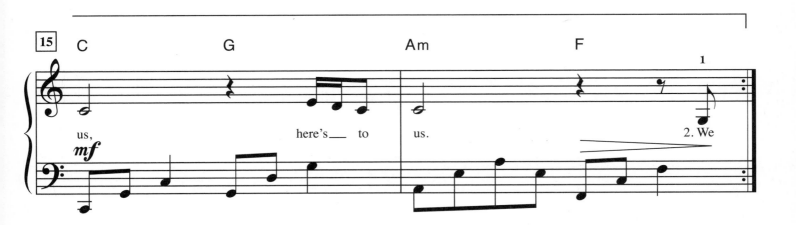

*Verse 2:*
We stuck it out this far together,
Put our dreams through the shredder.
Let's toast, 'cause things got better.
And everything could change like that,
And all these years go by so fast,
But nothing lasts forever.
*(To Chorus:)*

# IF I DIE YOUNG

Words and Music by Kimberly Perry
Arranged by Dan Coates

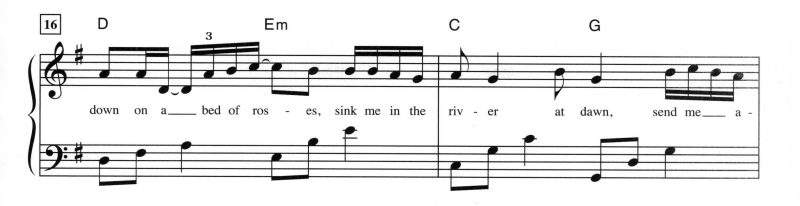

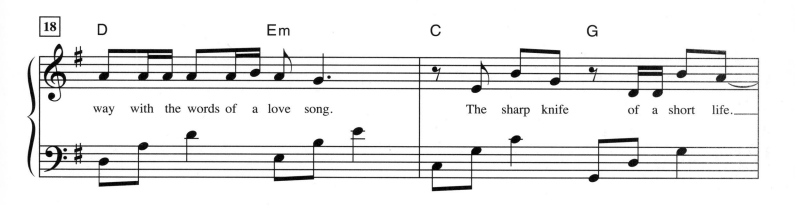

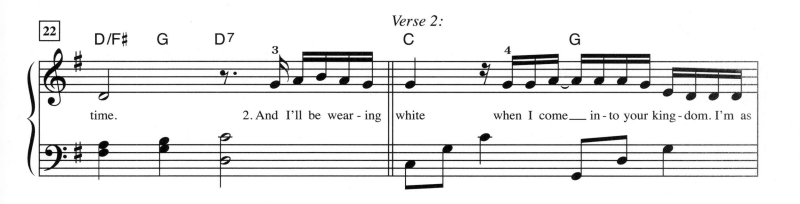

24

green as the ring on my lit-tle cold fin-ger. I've never known the lov - ing of a man, but it

sure felt nice when he was hold-ing my hand. There's a boy here in town, says he'll love me for-ev - er.

Who would have thought for-ev - er could be sev - ered by____ the sharp knife of a short life.____

_____ Well, I've____ had____ just e - nough time.____

*Bridge:*

So put on your best boys and I'll wear my pearls.

*Verse 3:*

*a tempo*

What I nev-er did is done. 3. A pen-ny for my thoughts, oh no, I'll sell them for a dol-lar.

*rit.*

# IT WILL RAIN

Words and Music by
Bruno Mars, Philip Lawrence and Ari Levine
Arranged by Dan Coates

There's no re-li-gion that could save me,_____

no mat-ter how long my knees are on the floor.

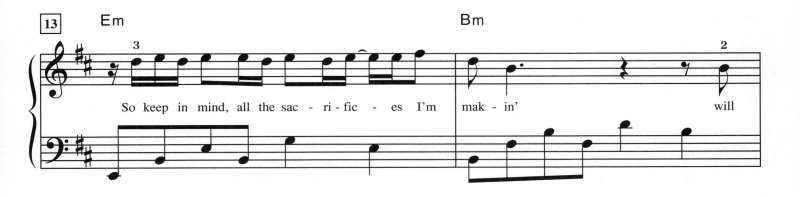

So keep in mind, all the sac-ri-fic-es I'm mak-in'      will

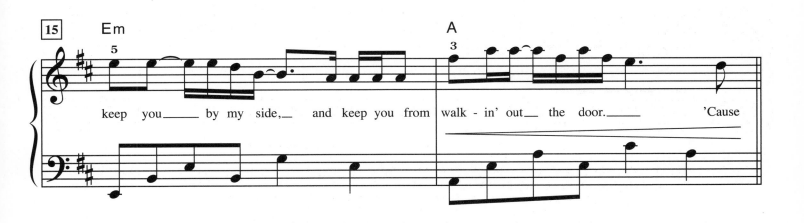

keep you_____ by my side,___ and keep you from walk-in' out___ the door._____ 'Cause

*Chorus:*

*Verse 2:*
I'll never be your mother's favorite,
Your daddy can't even look me in the eye.
If I was in their shoes, I'd be doin' the same thing.
Sayin', "There goes my little girl walkin' with that troublesome guy."
But they're just afraid of something they can't understand,
But little darling, watch me change their minds.
Yeah, for you, I'll try, I'll try, I'll try, I'll try.
I'll pick up these broken pieces 'til I'm bleeding,
If that'll make you mine.
*(To Chorus:)*

# JAR OF HEARTS

Words and Music by
Drew Lawrence, Christina Perri and Barrett Yeretsian
Arranged by Dan Coates

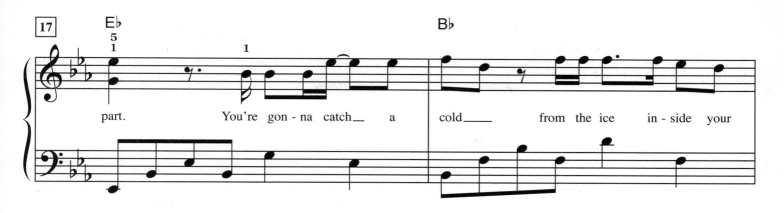

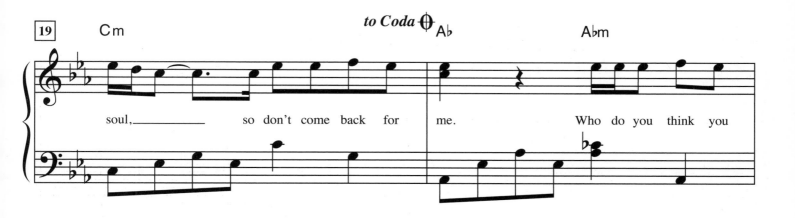

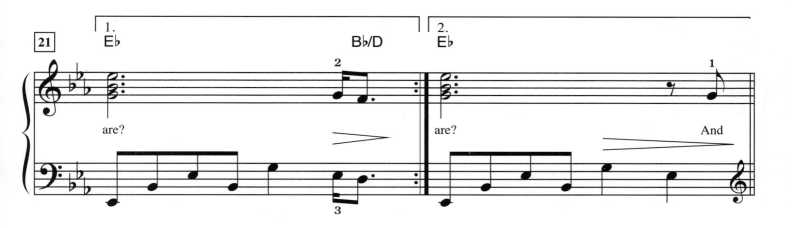

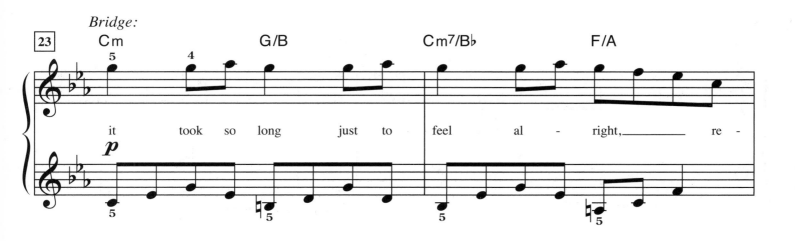

*Verse 2:*
I hear you're asking all around
If I am anywhere to be found.
But I have grown too strong
To ever fall back in your arms.
And I learned to live half alive,
And now you want me one more time.
*(To Chorus:)*

# LET ME BE YOUR STAR

Lyrics by Scott Wittman and Marc Shaiman
Music by Marc Shaiman
Arranged by Dan Coates

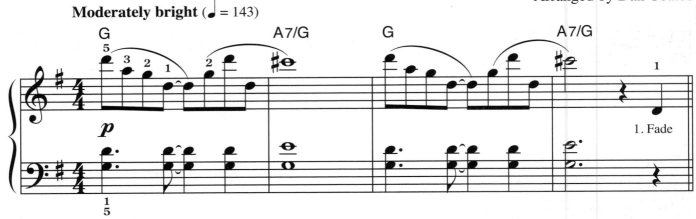

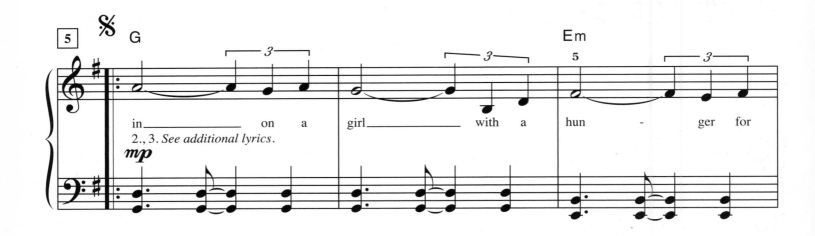

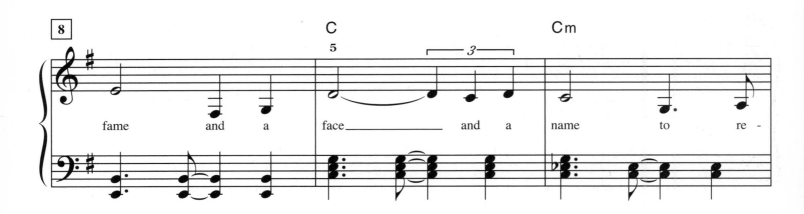

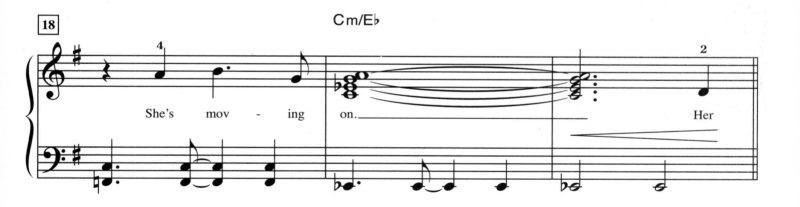

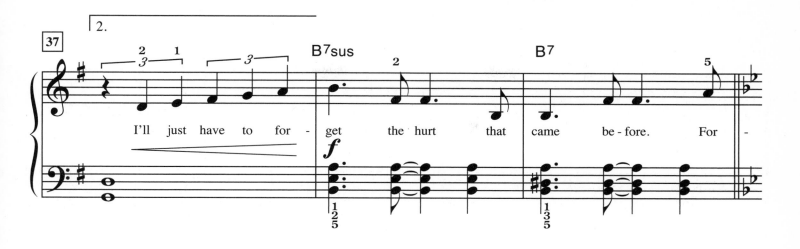

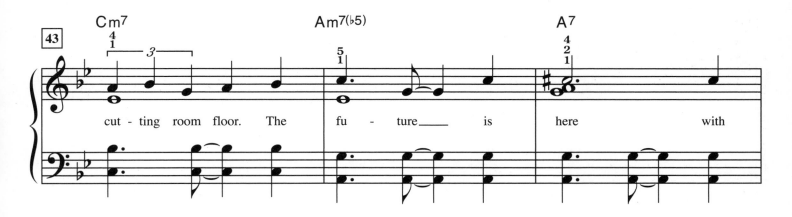

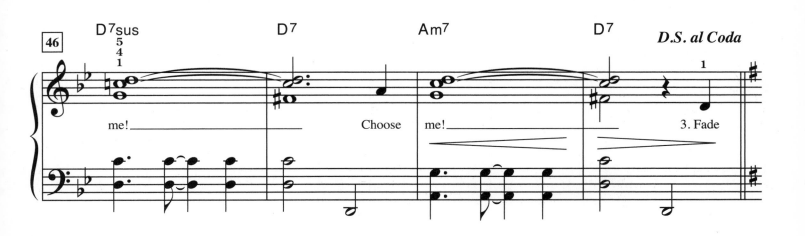

42

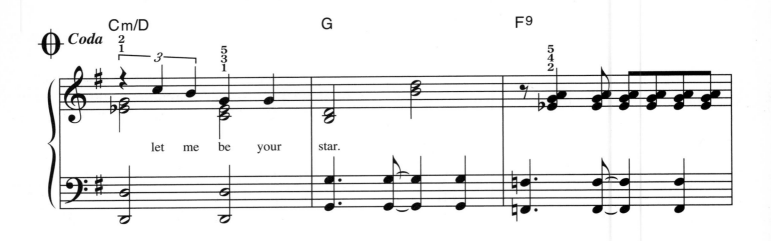

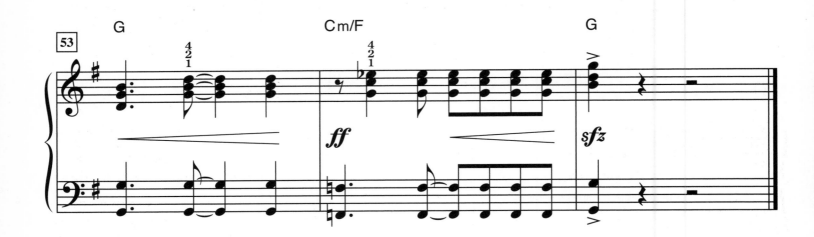

*Verse 2:*
Flash back to a girl with a song in her heart
As she's waiting to start the adventure.
The fire and drive that make dreams come alive,
They fill her soul. She's in control.
The drama, the laughter, the tears just like pearls,
Well, they're all in this girl's repertoire.
It's all for the taking and it's magic we'll be making,
Let me be your star.

*Verse 3:*
Fade up on a star with it all in her sights,
All the love and the lights that surround her.
Someday she'll think twice of the dues and the price
She'll have to pay, but not today!
She'll do all she can for the love of one man
And for millions who love from afar.
I'm what you've been needing, it's all here and her heart's pleading,
Let me be your star.

# LOVE YOU LIKE A LOVE SONG

Words and Music by
Antonina Armato, Adam Schmalholz and Tim James
Arranged by Dan Coates

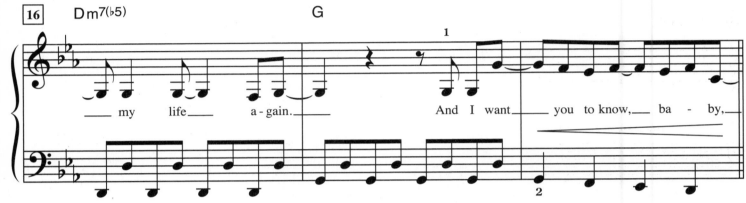

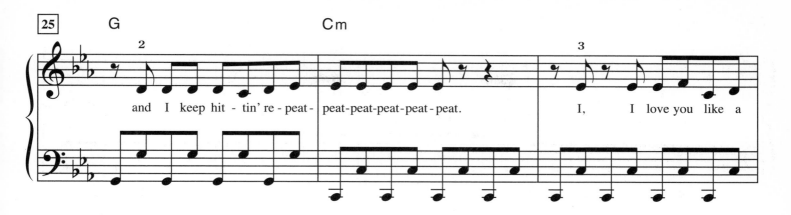

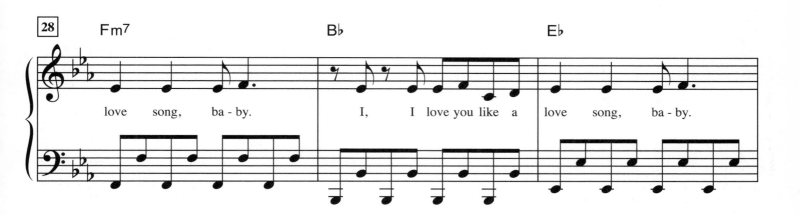

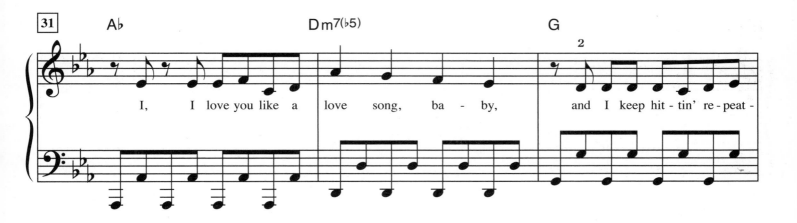

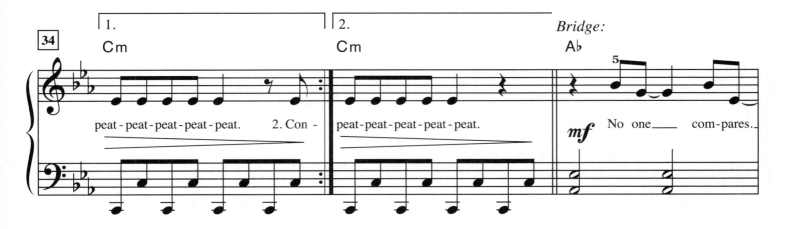

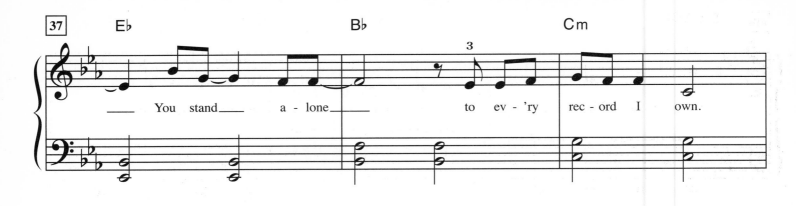

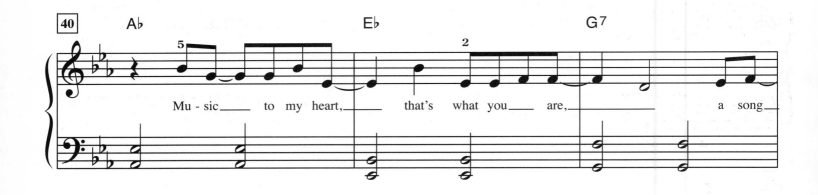

*Chorus:*

*Verse 2:*
Constantly, boy, you played through my mind like a symphony.
There's no way to describe what you do to me,
You just do to me what you do.
And it feels like I've been rescued, I've been set free.
I am hypnotized by your destiny.
You are magical, lyrical, beautiful.
You are. And I want you to know, baby,
*(To Chorus:)*

# NOT OVER YOU

Words and Music by
Gavin Degraw and Ryan Tedder
Arranged by Dan Coates

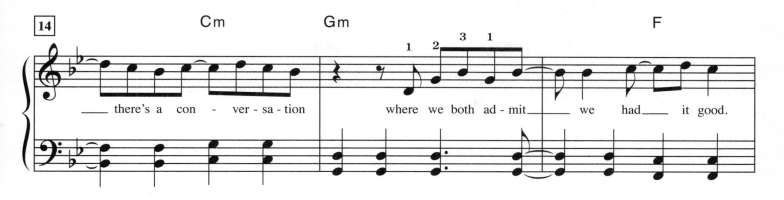

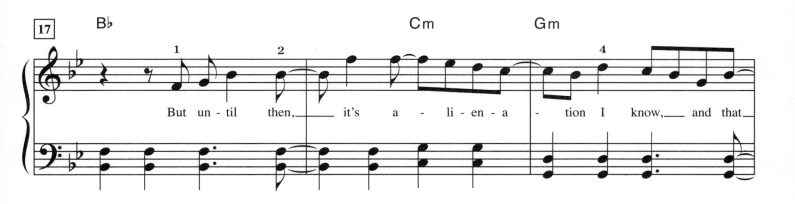

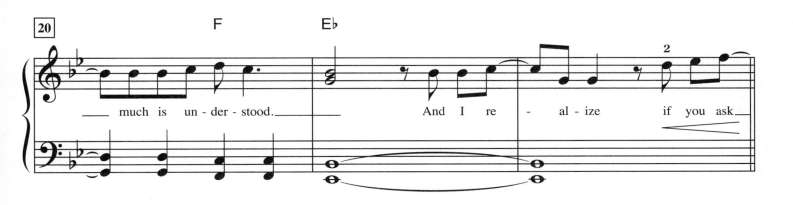

𝄋 *Chorus:*

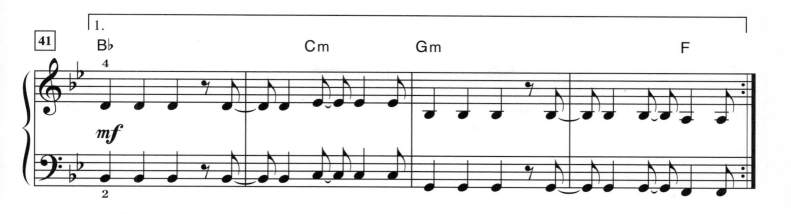

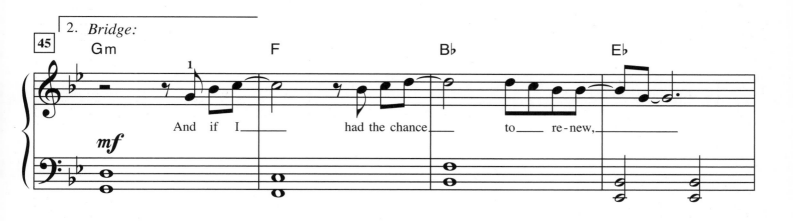

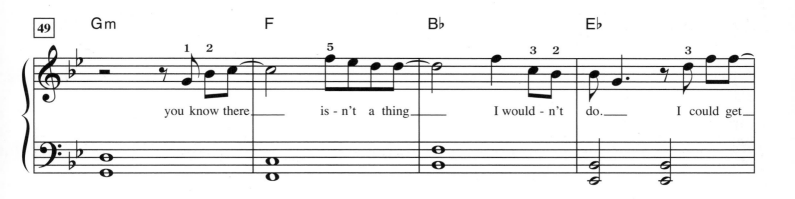

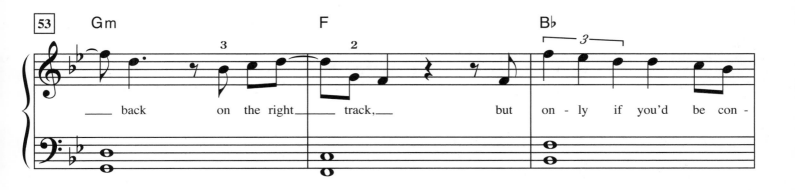

*Verse 2:*
Damn, damn, girl, you do it well.
And I thought you were innocent.
Took this heart and put it through hell,
But still, you're magnificent.
I, I'm a boomerang.
Doesn't matter how you throw me,
Turn around, and I'm back in the game,
Even better than the old me.
But I'm not even close without you.
*(To Chorus:)*

# PART OF ME

Words and Music by
Katy Perry, Lukasz Gottwald,
Max Martin and Bonnie McKee
Arranged by Dan Coates

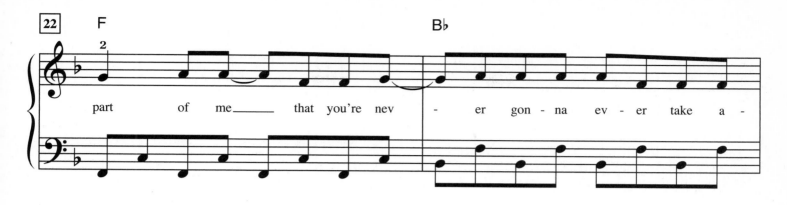

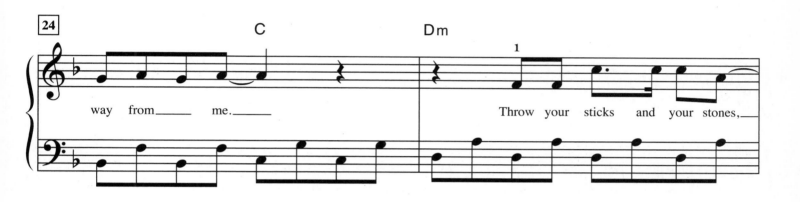

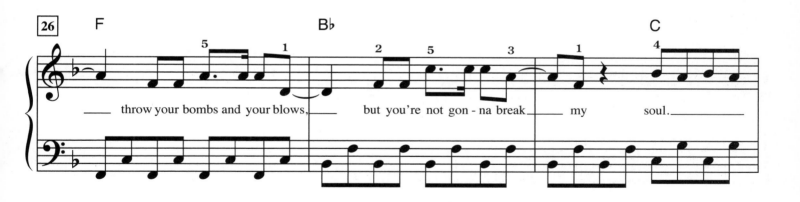

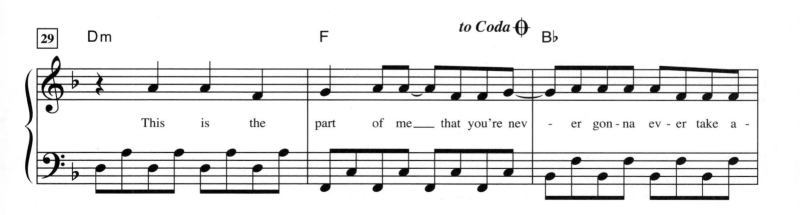

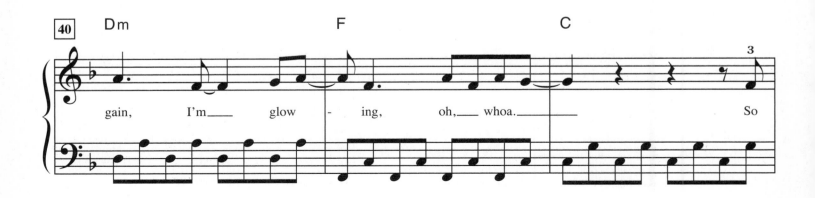

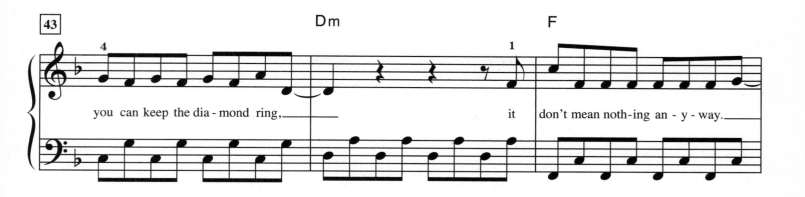

you can keep the dia-mond ring,_____ it don't mean noth-ing an - y - way._____

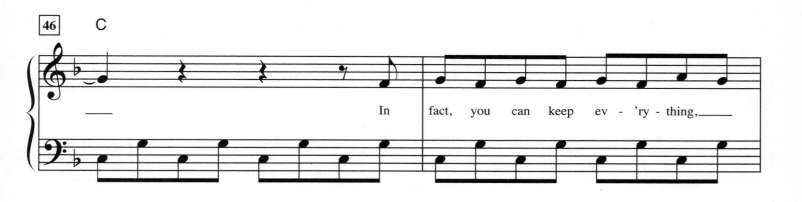

_____ In fact, you can keep ev - 'ry - thing,_____

D.S. al Coda

yeah,_____ yeah,_____ ex - cept for me.

Coda

- er gon - na ev - er take a - way from_____ me,_____ no._____

# SOME NIGHTS

Words and Music by
Nate Ruess, Andrew Dost,
Jack Antonoff and Jeffrey Bhasker
Arranged by Dan Coates

**Moderately, with a steady beat** (♩ = 108)

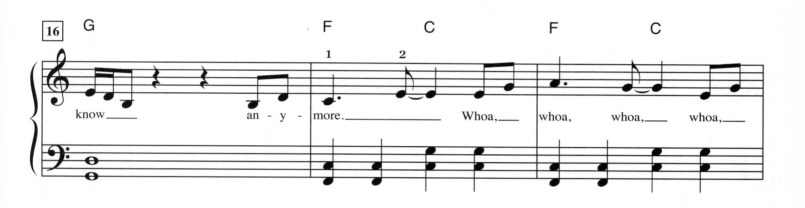

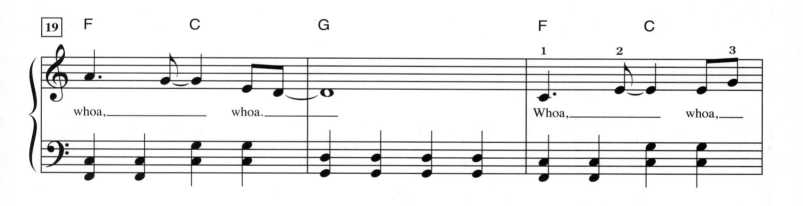

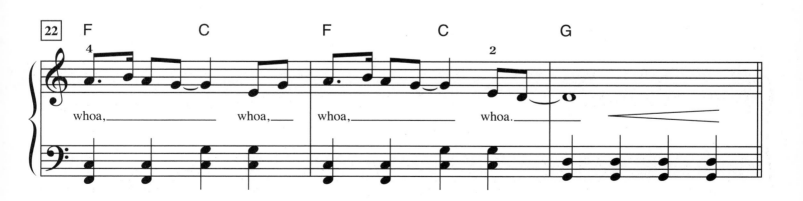

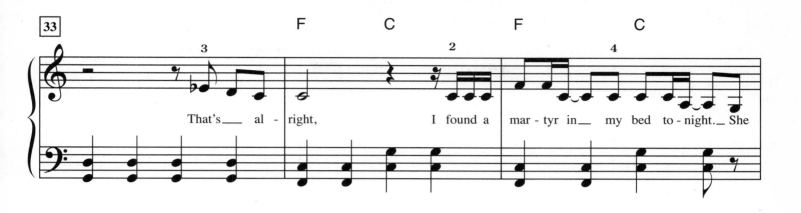

That's___ al - right, I found a mar - tyr in___ my bed to - night.___ She

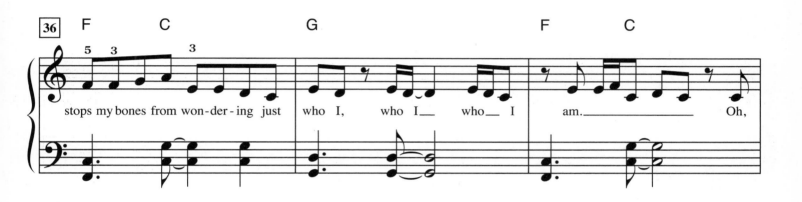

stops my bones from won-der - ing just who I, who I___ who___ I am._____ Oh,

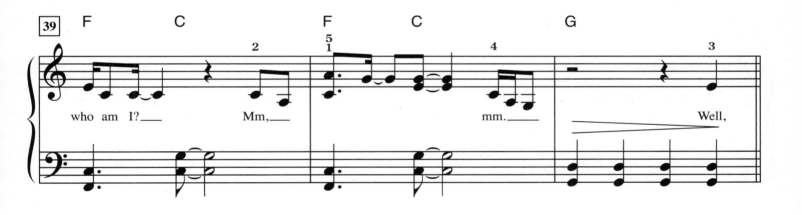

who am I?___ Mm,___ mm.___ Well,

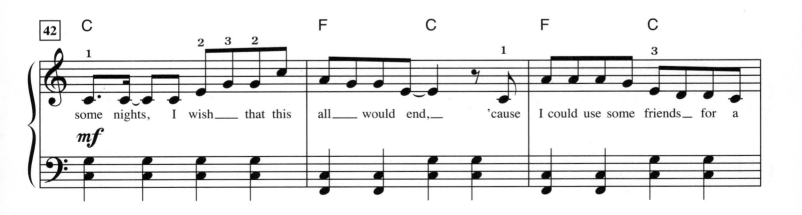

some nights, I wish___ that this all___ would end,___ 'cause I could use some friends___ for a

*mf*

**45** G / C / F / C

change. And some nights, I'm scared__ you'll for - get me__ a - gain,__ some

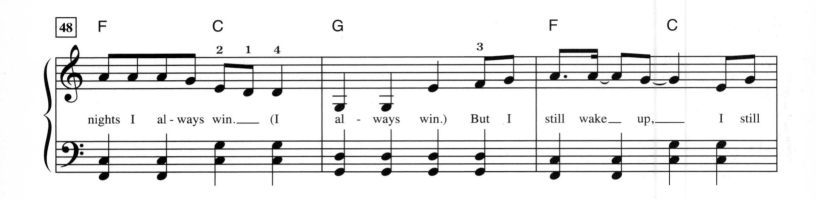

**48** F / C / G / F / C

nights I al - ways win.__ (I al - ways win.) But I still wake__ up,__ I still

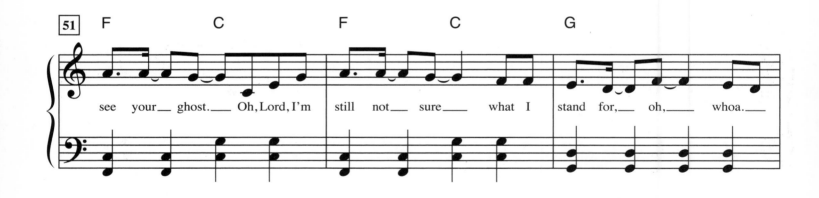

**51** F / C / F / C / G

see your__ ghost.__ Oh, Lord, I'm still not__ sure__ what I stand for,__ oh,__ whoa.__

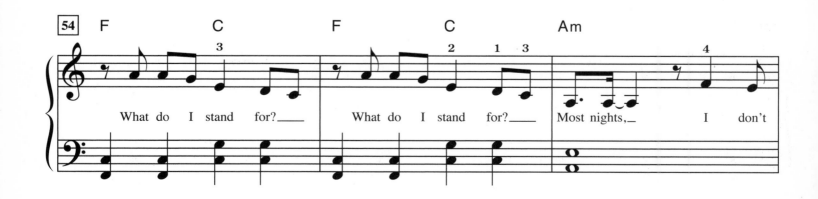

**54** F / C / F / C / Am

What do I stand for?__ What do I stand for?__ Most nights,__ I don't

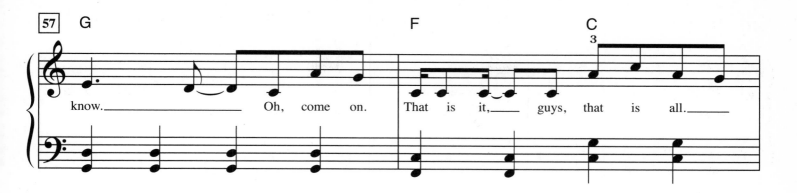

know._____ Oh, come on. That is it,\_\_\_\_ guys, that is all.\_\_\_\_\_

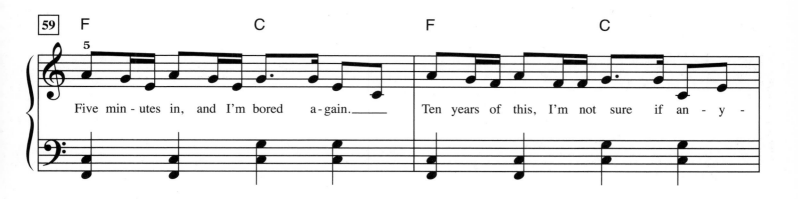

Five min - utes in, and I'm bored a - gain.\_\_\_\_\_ Ten years of this, I'm not sure if an - y -

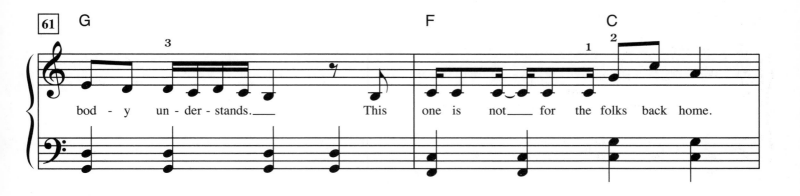

bod - y un - der - stands.\_\_\_\_ This one is not\_\_\_\_ for the folks back home.

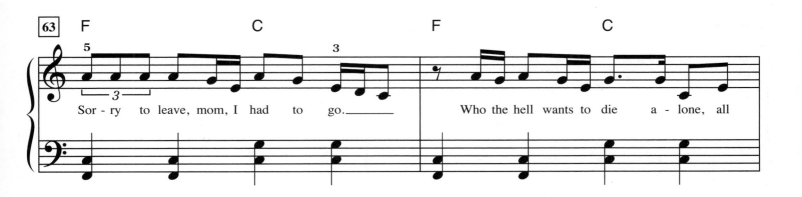

Sor - ry to leave, mom, I had to go._____ Who the hell wants to die a - lone, all

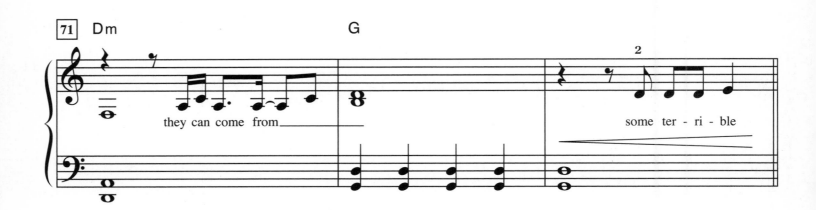

# WE ARE YOUNG

Words and Music by
Nate Ruess, Andrew Dost,
Jack Antonoff and Jeffrey Bhasker
Arranged by Dan Coates

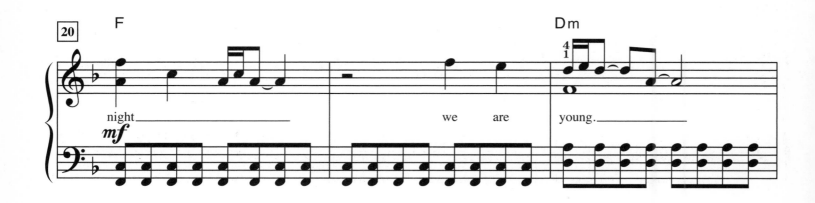

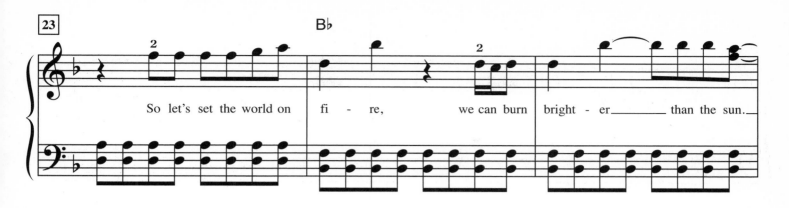

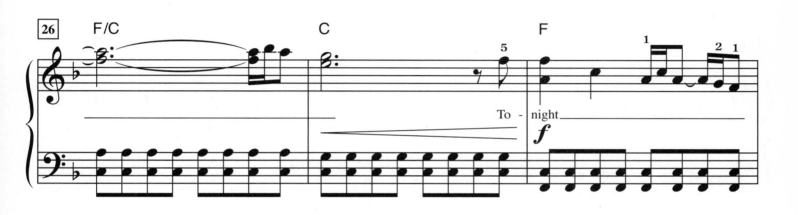

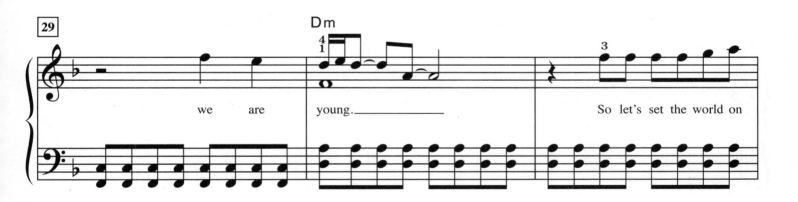

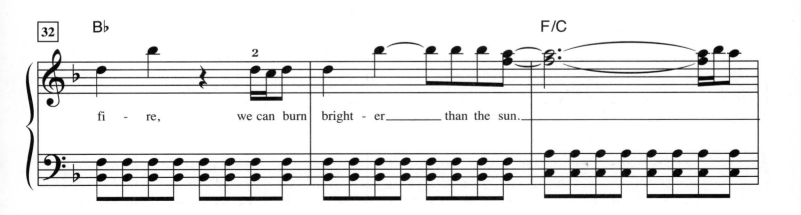

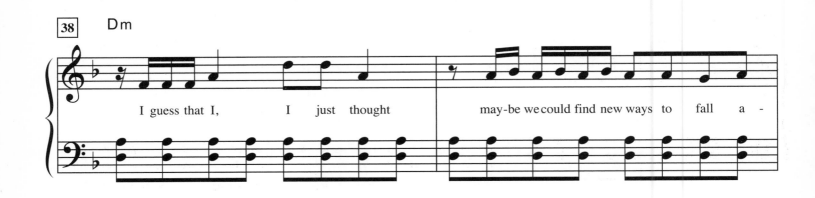

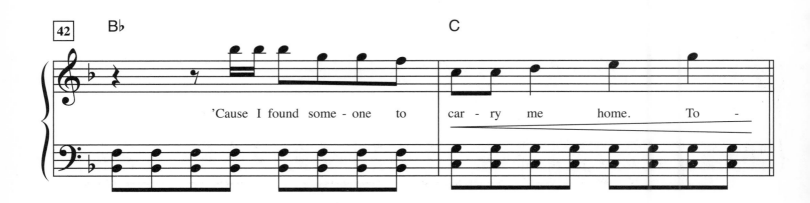

night_____

we are young._____

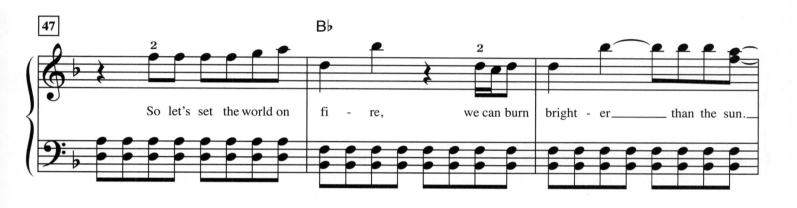

So let's set the world on fi - re, we can burn bright - er_____ than the sun.

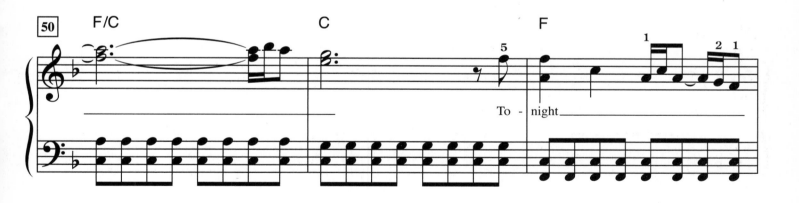

_____ To - night_____

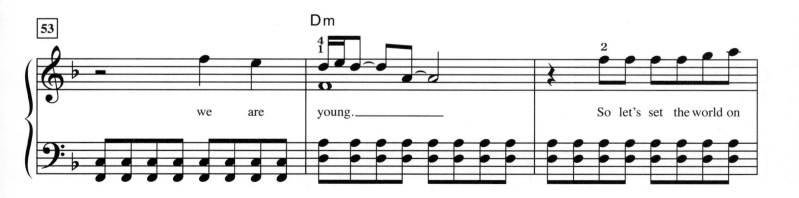

we are young._____ So let's set the world on

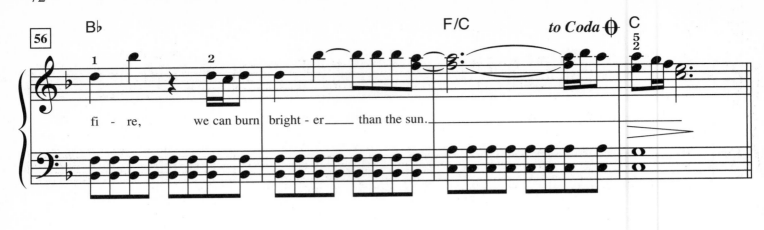

fi - re,  we can burn bright - er_____ than the sun._____

Car - ry me home to - night,_____ just car - ry me home to - night.

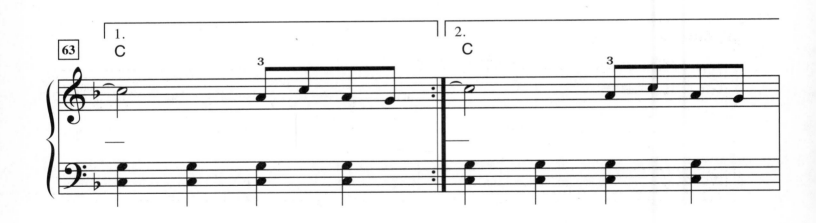

_____ The world is on my side, I have no rea-son to run. So will some-one come and

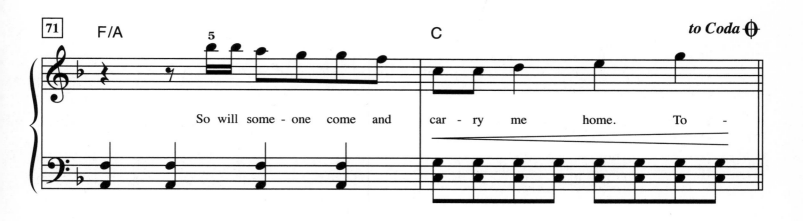

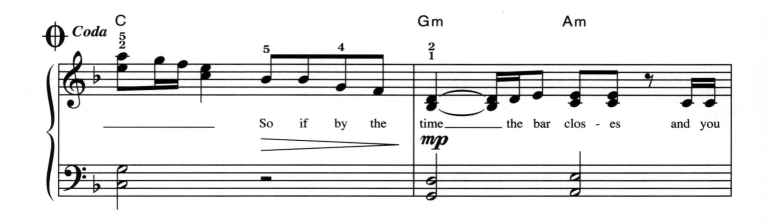

# SOMEBODY THAT I USED TO KNOW

Words by Walter DeBacker
Music by Luiz Bonfa
Arranged by Dan Coates

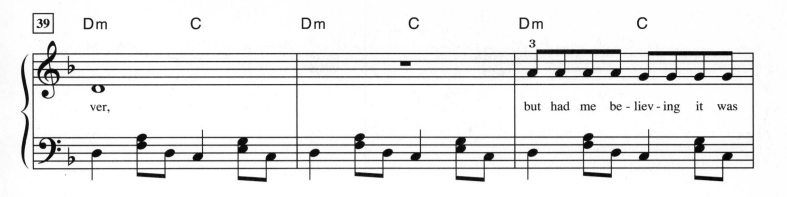

ver, but had me be - liev - ing it was

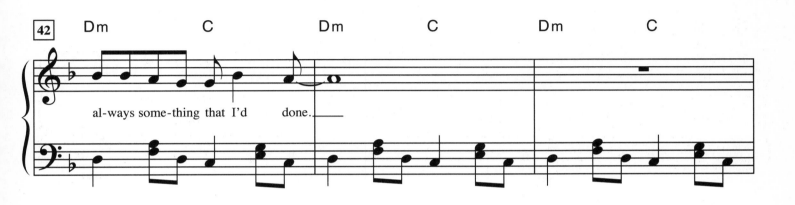

al - ways some - thing that I'd done.

But I don't wan - na live that way, read - ing in - to ev - 'ry

word you say. You said that you could let it go,___ and I